FOOTBALL LEGENDS

Troy Aikman

Terry Bradshaw

Jim Brown

John Elway

Brett Favre

Michael Irvin

Vince Lombardi

John Madden

Dan Marino

Joe Montana

Joe Namath

Walter Payton

Jerry Rice

Barry Sanders

Deion Sanders

Emmitt Smith

Lawrence Taylor

Steve Young

CHELSEA HOUSE PUBLISHERS

FOOTBALL LEGENDS

LAWRENCE TAYLOR

Dan Hirshberg

Introduction by
Chuck Noll

CHELSEA HOUSE PUBLISHERS
Philadelphia

Produced by Daniel Bial and Associates
New York, New York

Picture research by Alan Gottlieb
Cover illustration by Earl Parker

First Printing

1 3 5 7 9 8 6 4 2

Library of Congress Cataloging-in-Publication Data

Hirshberg, Dan.
    Lawrence Taylor / Dan Hirshberg; introduction by Chuck Daly.
      p. cm. -- (Football legends)
    Includes bibiliographical references and index.
    Summary: A biography which focuses on the football career of the
    star linebacker for the New York Giants, Lawrence Taylor, also known
    as "L.T."
    ISBN 0-7910-4429-7
    1. Taylor, Lawrence, 1959- --Juvenile literature. 2. Football
players--United States--Biography--Juvenile literature. 3. New York
Giants (Football team)--Juvenile literature.   [1. Taylor, Lawrence,
1959- . 2. Football players. 3. Afro-Americans--Biography.]
I. Title. II. Series.
GV939. T34H57   1997
796.332'092--dc21
[B]   97-14225
                                                  CIP
                                                  AC

CONTENTS

A WINNING ATTITUDE   6
Chuck Noll

CHAPTER 1
LEADER ON THE FIELD   9

CHAPTER 2
PITTSBURGH, HERE I COME   15

CHAPTER 3
EARNING A REP   23

CHAPTER 4
NEW YORK, NEW YORK   31

CHAPTER 5
SUPERHUMAN AND
ALL TOO HUMAN   39

CHAPTER 6
ONE OF THE GREATS   51

STATISTICS   61
CHRONOLOGY   62
FURTHER READING   63
INDEX   64

A WINNING ATTITUDE

Chuck Noll

Don't ever fall into the trap of believing, "I could never do that. And I won't even try—I don't want to embarrass myself." After all, most top athletes had no idea what they could accomplish when they were young. A secret to the success of every star quarterback and sure-handed receiver is that they tried. If they had not tried, if they had not persevered, they would never have discovered how far they could go and how much they could achieve.

You can learn about trying hard and overcoming challenges by being a sports fan. Or you can take part in organized sports at any level, in any capacity. The student messenger at my high school is now president of a university. A reserve ballplayer who got very little playing time in high school now owns a very successful business. Both of them benefited by the lesson of perseverance that sports offers. The main point is that you don't have to be a Hall of Fame athlete to reap the benefits of participating in sports.

In math class, I learned that the whole is equal to the sum of its parts. But that is not always the case when you are dealing with people. Sports has taught me that the whole is either greater than or less than the sum of its parts, depending on how well the parts work together. And how the parts work together depends on how they really understand the concept of teamwork.

Most people believe that teamwork is a fifty-fifty proposition. But true teamwork is seldom, if ever, fifty-fifty. Teamwork is *whatever it takes to get the job done*. There is no time for the measurement of contributions, no time for anything but concentrating on your job.

One year, my Pittsburgh Steelers were playing the Houston

Oilers in the Astrodome late in the season, with the division championship on the line. Our offensive line was hard hit by the flu, our starting quarterback was out with an injury, and we were having difficulty making a first down. There was tremendous pressure on our defense to perform well—and they rose to the occasion. If the players on the defensive unit had been measuring their contribution against the offense's contribution, they would have given up and gone home. Instead, with a "whatever it takes" attitude, they increased their level of concentration and performance, forced turnovers, and got the ball into field goal range for our offense. Thanks to our defense's winning attitude, we came away with a victory.

Believing in doing whatever it takes to get the job done is what separates a successful person from someone who is not as successful. Nobody can give you this winning outlook; you have to develop it. And I know from experience that it can be learned and developed on the playing field.

My favorite people on the football field have always been offensive linemen and defensive backs. I say this because it takes special people to perform well in jobs in which there is little public recognition when they are doing things right but are thrust into the spotlight as soon as they make a mistake. That is exactly what happens to a lineman whose man sacks the quarterback or a defensive back who lets his receiver catch a touchdown pass. They know the importance of being part of a group that believes in teamwork and does not point fingers at one another.

Sports can be a learning situation as much as it can be fun. And that's why I say, "Get involved. Participate."

CHUCK NOLL, the Pittsburgh Steelers head coach from 1969–1991, led his team to four Super Bowl victories—the most by any coach. Widely respected as an innovator on both offense and defense, Noll was inducted into the Pro Football Hall of Fame in 1993.

1

LEADER ON THE FIELD

The 1990 season started out like a dream for both Lawrence Taylor and the New York Giants. When the Big Blue blanked the Detroit Lions, 20-0, they enjoyed a gaudy 10-0 record. But then they lost road games to the Philadelphia Eagles, 31-13, and to the San Francisco 49ers, 7-3, in a Monday night encounter that had people on the east coast falling asleep as the Giants mounted little offense. Back at home, in windy Giants Stadium on December 9, they were struggling to score points, let alone win a ball game as they faced the red-hot Minnesota Vikings.

The Giants defense was ranked first in the National Football League. And New York was a shoo-in for a wild card berth. But these were the Giants, the big bad Giants, and the fans made it known they weren't happy about the prospect of the team sneaking into the playoffs as a wild card. Thoughts of clinching their second straight

Lawrence Taylor's sheer presence could inspire his team—and rattle his opponents—even when he was off the field.

NFC Eastern Division crown, however, were fast fading away as the team slumped.

The Giants had a good quarterback, a fine offensive line, several terrific linebackers, and one undisputed star, Lawrence Taylor. LT, a one-man demolition crew, did things no linebacker had done before. He chased down running backs from behind. He took on three blockers and still tackled the ball carrier. He smacked the ball out of backs' hands to cause fumbles. He covered tight ends and made interceptions. And above all, he sacked quarterbacks. No matter how big or how fast the blocker was, LT found a way to get through to the passer and grind his face in the dirt.

But fans were now wondering if LT's career was beginning to fade away. The Giants' 31-year-old superstar linebacker had seemed a bit slower the past few weeks. The years of being double- and triple-teamed, of having offenses geared strictly to stop him, had seemingly taken its toll on him. The press was starting to say that Taylor's days were numbered. And even Taylor admitted after the Philly game that he was feeling "slower," that maybe he wasn't as fast as he once had been. So concerned was he that he went on a diet, looking to find that extra step again.

In the first half, Herschel Walker ran roughshod over the Giants defense, rushing for 78 of his team's 175 first half yards. Even though the score was relatively low at the break, with the Giants down 12-10, the Giant's vaunted defense had played nothing like the highly-touted unit that they were considered to be. The Vikings, fighting to earn a wild-card playoff bid for themselves, were in control of the game.

Taylor sacks Vikings' quarter-back Rich Gannon and forces him to fumble the ball in this 1990 game.

In the Giant's locker room, coaches and players went over offensive and defensive schemes as they searched for answers. Minutes before the break was over, Taylor had made an announcement. He had never been comfortable with his role as co-captain, preferring to let his actions on the field speak for him. But now, with sweat still pouring down his face and his uniform smudged with dirt, he addressed his teammates. "We're not physical enough," he said. "We've got to start gang-tackling. I'm going to start playing the way we're supposed to play. If anybody wants to come along, that's fine." He looked around the room and added, "We've got 30 minutes to win the division."

When the second half began, the New York defense immediately took control. As if taking a cue from his own speech, Taylor was in quarterback Rich Gannon's face from the first play of the second half to the last. Many were the quarterbacks who had looked into Taylor's eyes before taking the snap and known the meaning of the word fear. "LT had Rich Gannon looking left to see if LT was coming and if Gannon saw LT, he was running," said Giants safety Greg Jackson.

The Giants' defense pressed Minnesota and finally in the fourth quarter, with the Giants behind 15-10, the pressure began to pay off in big dividends. On the opening play of the last quarter, Jackson intercepted a Gannon pass deep in Viking territory, and Matt Bahr's 33-yard field goal four plays later brought the Giants to within two points. New York stopped Minnesota cold on its next possession, with Taylor and rookie lineman Mike Fox combining to sack Gannon on a crucial down to pin the Vikings back to their own 10. "Just keep hittin' them, just keep hittin' them," Taylor kept exhorting in the defensive huddle. "Fifteen minutes to the divisional championship!"

A short punt and eight plays later, Ottis Anderson, who would go over 10,000 career rushing yards that day, bulled over from the 2 yard line for a 20-15 Giants lead. And not long after, a blitzing Taylor hurried Gannon into a pass that was picked off by linebacker Gary Reasons to set up a game-clinching 18-yard field goal by Bahr.

"When you make a quarterback throw higher, you can get an interception," said Reasons. "Lawrence made him throw higher."

In the visitors' locker room afterwards, Gannon, whose team was effectively eliminated from the playoffs, shook his head. "That one-man wrecking crew, LT, played a great fourth quarter," he said.

When it was over, Taylor, who had been wondering himself a few weeks earlier what he had left, had made nine tackles, had three assists, 2½ sacks, one forced fumble, and one forced interception. Not merely had Lawrence Taylor and company kept the Vikings to three points of offense in the second half, they had effectively positioned the Giants' offense so it could score 10 points with relative ease.

In the home team's locker room, Taylor refused to take credit for the Giants' second half revival. "I don't know what I said at halftime, I really don't," he told a swarm of reporters as they pressed close to his locker to record his every word. "I just talk. If they listen, they listen." As for his own assault, he declared, "I just do it. Once I get into the game I don't see a whole lot of what goes on out there."

Coach Bill Parcells, who had spent the night before in a hospital with a painful kidney stone, simply shrugged his shoulders. "He won't let us lose," he said. "Nothing that guy does surprises me. He's a great, great player—the best defensive player over the last 10 years and it's not close for second."

Instead of losing their third straight, the Giants were back on track and on their way toward a Super Bowl victory over the Buffalo Bills several weeks later, their second Super Bowl crown in five years. Taylor, honored as the NFC Defensive Player of the Week, played a big role in the win, leading, in this case, not only on the field, but in an unfamiliar role as team spokesman. And, as it turned out, there were many other great games left in Taylor.

2

PITTSBURGH, HERE I COME

As a youngster growing up on the outskirts of Williamsburg, Virginia, Lawrence Taylor showed no particular signs that he would some-day become a great football player. That's because Taylor never played organized football until he was in high school. He played in backyard pick-up games, but that was about it. Actually, Taylor didn't care for football as a youngster. He didn't watch it on television, didn't read about it in the newspapers.

Now baseball, that was something else. Taylor played on a number of teams and that was where he made an early name for himself. While most kids avoid the catcher position like the plague, Taylor relished wearing the "tools of igno-rance." Nobody blocked the plate better on a play at home and nobody could stop pitches in the dirt any better. And he could hit the ball hard. Taylor might have got some of that baseball spunk from his father, who was a pretty good

In high school, Robin Canady and Lawrence Taylor were voted the most athletic students.

player himself and who regularly played with a softball team called the Toano Giants.

As a child, Taylor spent a lot of time by himself. He grew up in a small house in the woods near a busy two-lane highway. There were neighbors, but not right next door. Taylor is one of three boys, with Buddy the oldest and Kim the youngest. His parents were hard-working people. Clarence, his father, worked at the shipyards in Newport News, leaving for work before dawn. Iris, his mother, worked several different odd jobs over the years, as well, doing whatever was necessary to bring in extra money so that the family could eat a good meal every day and to ensure that everyone had clothes on their back. The extra money was nice—and necessary—but it also meant that the boys often spent time with babysitters, and when they were old enough, by themselves. Because of that, and because of where they lived, Lawrence and his brothers spent a great deal of time on their own. To this day, even though he is one of the most famous people in the country and has played football before thousands of fans, Taylor has never become fully comfortable around lots of people.

The family had strong religious ties. Lawrence and his brothers regularly went to church and Sunday school. He even sang in the church choir. At the end of the week on Friday night, his mother gathered the boys around for family discussions. They would talk about everything from what went on that week in school to God. "She taught us to be God-fearing, to make something of ourselves, to believe in ourselves," Taylor recalls in his autobiography. The talks helped Taylor, who never missed a day of class through high school, become a pretty good student.

The talks may have helped Taylor think big. He once "borrowed" some money from his mother and bought a lot of candy. The next day he went to school and sold the goodies at a profit. He paid his mother back and with the money left over bought some more candy. Soon, he was known as the "Candy Man" at school.

Another time Taylor "borrowed" his father's bicycle. Only this time, he got into deep trouble. He blew a tire on the bike and crushed a wheel. After ditching the bike in some woods he went home and of course, his father was upset over the bike's disappearance. Lawrence didn't say a word and his father couldn't pin the blame on anyone since no one was talking. The next day, the 11-year-old figured he'd "borrow" his father's truck, pick up the bike, and find a bike shop that could make the repairs. Taylor—driving in first gear all the way—somehow made it to downtown Williamsburg three miles away. In the process, however, the truck broke down in the middle of a main street. Never one to give up, though, Taylor found a mechanic who agreed to fix the truck. When the mechanic found out Taylor had no money to pay for the repairs, the two agreed on a payoff. The youngster would mow the mechanic's lawn. While it took all Saturday to mow the lawn, Taylor was relieved.

One day, when he was 15, Taylor was shagging fly balls one early autumn day when he noticed a bunch of kids playing football on the next field. Before he knew it, the coach of that football team, Pete Babcock, came over and asked the high school sophomore if he'd like to play for his Williamsburg Jaycee squad. Taylor balked at the offer but soon learned that the team would be traveling to Pittsburgh to play another Jaycee team later in the year. Taylor had never had much chance to travel, so he said okay.

The coach told him he'd be playing linebacker, but Taylor didn't know much about football. In order to learn about his new position, he went to the library and took out books on how to play linebacker.

Taylor had visions of remaining with the Jaycees during his junior year at what was practically a brand new Lafayette High School, but an assistant coach, Melvin Jones, prodded Taylor to join the high school team. But Taylor was hesitant. He was 5' 8", 180 pounds, and didn't know if he was good enough to even make the strong Lafayette football team, let alone start.

"The coaches sort of convinced him to play," remembers Betsy Thomas, Taylor's former homeroom teacher and now Lafayette's Director of Athletics. "They pursued him, told him he ought to be playing."

Taylor's early days on the team were tough on him. He was just another player during two-a-day preseason workouts and he was regularly getting banged around. When the season started, Taylor took his place on the bench, fearful, he says in his autobiography, of what lay ahead. "I'd sit on the bench, scared and praying that I wouldn't be sent in." At one practice, he couldn't take it anymore and walked off the field, telling no one in particular that he quit. But Jones chased him down and talked Taylor into sticking it out.

Over the first few weeks, the coaches tried Taylor out at center, guard, tackle, and eventually end, both on offense and defense. They had him second on the depth chart all along but sensed he had potential.

"I didn't know a lot about him," says Mike Bucci, Lafayette's head football coach back then. "I knew he was an athlete, that he loved baseball. When he came out for us he was fairly big, 185-190, and because he was a big fella we started him on the interior line."

Taylor didn't play one minute of a varsity ball game the first four weeks. In the fifth week, though, his football life suddenly took shape. It was a rainy, cold Friday night at Cooley Field and Lafayette was hosting archrival Bethel. A crowd of close to 10,000 was on hand as the two teams fought it out in a defensive struggle through the first half. One of Lafayette's defensive ends, meanwhile, was having his problems and finally, Bucci wanted a change. "Taylor, get ready!" he yelled.

After a few good plays, a nervous Taylor started to get more comfortable. In the fourth quarter, the score still 0-0, Bethel faced a fourth-down punting situation. Taylor rushed hard at the snap and leaped high in the air. His right hand got a piece of the ball and it fell into the arms of teammate Tony McConnel who sprinted into the end zone for what proved to be the winning score in a 6-0 finale.

The next day Taylor, already feeling pretty good, went to downtown Williamsburg. He was amazed at the reception he got. Wherever he went people congratulated him. They shook his hand, high-fived him and clearly were excited for him. As if that wasn't enough, Taylor picked up a newspaper and saw his name in the headline and all over the sports pages!

"He played very well in that fifth game," recalls Bucci. "He had the blocked punt and made some good plays. That was the beginning for him. He won a starting position and he got better and better every game."

Taylor improved day in and day out. By his senior year, he was really ready to make some noise and that he did. He got a reputation as one of the area's top players, making the area all-star team, and began to make a mark for himself as a quarterback's worst nightmare. He had several big games as a senior, catching touchdown passes as a tight end and making a huge sack on a quarterback from his defensive end post.

Bucci remembered one game in particular. "We were battling Hampton High School, a team that is always ranked in the nation. We beat them in 1973 and 1974 and they won in 1975. Now it's 1976, Lawrence's senior year, and it's early in the season. It was pretty even at halftime until he turned the game around. It started with a punting play and Lawrence blocked it. It hit somebody's shoulder pad and Taylor caught it in stride and ran it in for a touchdown. He caught two other touchdowns and had a number of sacks. He really played a game that day."

Although Bucci didn't know a lot about Taylor prior to his first practice, over time, he appreciated what Taylor had to offer. "He always had a lot of natural ability," says Bucci. "And he was easy to teach. You didn't have to tell him some-

This photograph taken at a reunion shows assistant coach Mel Jones (left), who talked Lawrence Taylor (second from right) into attending Lafayette High School. Jones compared Taylor to Ron Springs (second from left) who also starred at Lafayette and later went on to a pro career. At center is assistant coach Mark Anderson and head coach Mike Bucci is at right.

thing twice. That carried over into his senior year and helped him have an outstanding year. When I later saw him play in college and in the pros it was very easy to look back and say I saw that he had the ability in high school. Of course, while I knew he could go beyond high school I didn't know he'd be tops at his position."

As good a senior season as Taylor had had, his future still remained up in the air. Since he had gotten a late start with high school football, he found himself behind the eight ball with big-time college recruiters. He did get the usual letters, but mostly from small schools or junior colleges. Both Bucci and his assistant Jones were convinced that Taylor could play on a major college team. It was a hard sell, though.

"I knew he was good, that he was good enough to play big-time college ball," says Bucci, who coached two other future NFL players, Ron Springs and Mel Gray. "But because he came on so late, he wasn't on any recruiting lists. It was hard to convince those folks. The feedback we were getting from schools was that he was just another big guy."

Eventually it came down to two schools. The University of Richmond recruited Taylor heavily and Taylor was leaning to attending there until the University of North Carolina caught wind of him. Mike Mansfield, a recruiter, met with Taylor a number of times and brought the teenager to Chapel Hill for a visit. North Carolina, with its academic excellence and tradition of sending graduates to the National Football League, wanted Taylor. And Taylor wanted to be a Tar Heel.

3
EARNING A REP

Coach Bill Dooley had been hesitant about signing Taylor to a scholarship. He considered Taylor a "sleeper" and he wanted to be sure he was making the right decision. In college football, you don't want to waste a scholarship on someone who *might* be good. Dooley needed to see some proof. By now, however, it was winter. Dooley couldn't see Taylor on the football field, so he figured he'd see what the kid had to offer on the basketball court.

"One of my assistants told me I had to come and look at this guy," recalls Dooley. "He was on the high school basketball team so I went to see him in a game. I watched him and immediately I thought, 'My gosh. He is big and strong and can move.' You don't always find that combination. He could move, that's what impressed me. He had the ability to accelerate. Shoot, I felt we could make him a football player if he had any kind of heart."

Although everyone recognized that he had talent, Taylor did not get to play very much during his first two years at the University of North Carolina.

The day Taylor took the field for the first practice, he didn't feel very confident. "Lafayette had 33, 35 guys on the football team," Taylor wrote in his book. "Carolina had over a hundred players and eight or nine coaches. Where I played both ways at Lafayette, here I was lucky to be playing at all. My first practice the sight of those Carolina players was just plain intimidating. I was 6'1", about 205 pounds—and I was small! Billy Johnson, our fullback, was 265 pounds. Dee Hardison was 280 or 290. The outside linebackers on the team, Kenny Sheets and T. K. McDaniels, were both around 6'6" and 230 pounds. I couldn't believe I was going to make it there. I kept telling myself, 'Who are you fooling?' That freshman year I didn't even want to get into any games."

Taylor not only had to get used to bigger players and rougher practices, but he also had to get used to a busier schedule. Not only were there two or three practices a day, but there were meetings, films, and schoolwork.

North Carolina was coming off a 9-3 season and featured a host of fine defensive players. For a time, the coaching staff argued over whether Taylor should play offense or defense. Eventually, the defensive coaches won and Taylor was pegged as an outside linebacker. And in short time, they were proved right.

"Taylor didn't play much his freshman year because we had a couple of really good linebackers," says Dooley. "So he would always be on our scout team [the team that lines up in the look of the opponent that particular week so that the first team can run its plays and get a feel of who they will be facing]. Two weeks into the season we couldn't move the ball against Lawrence.

Right then and there I knew he would be a good football player."

Carolina's 8-3-1 record won the Atlantic Coast Conference title and earned them a bid to the Liberty Bowl, which they lost to Nebraska. Taylor didn't get into any games, except as a special teams player. As the year went on, though, he gained confidence. Hardison told him one day, "You gonna be pretty good, son," a compliment that Taylor gladly accepted.

Off the field, Taylor was making a name for himself as a wild guy. To show his toughness, he ate glass on one occasion. Another time, he took the hard way to his dormitory room, climbing six stories up the side of the brick-faced building. By the time Taylor, who had gotten into more than a few scraps with the law, left UNC, he was aptly nicknamed "The Monster."

Prior to Taylor's second season, Dooley resigned to take the head football job at Virginia Tech. Dick Crum, the new coach, brought in his own staff, set up his own rules and was determined to make the UNC program his own. While Taylor was not a fan of Crum, he did earn a starting inside linebacker position his sophomore year. That role ended in a hurry, though, when Taylor broke a bone in his foot the first game of the year against East Carolina. By the time he was ready to get back into the lineup, Darrell Nicholson, who would become the ACC Rookie of the Year, was in his spot. The frustrated Taylor was in and out of the starting lineup, moving from inside linebacker to outside linebacker and to nose guard. Nagging injuries were no help, and his sophomore year ended on a down note. Taylor's numbers were uninspiring. He had no quarterback sacks, didn't force a fumble, and was in on a mere 28 tackles. The Tar Heels tumbled to 5-6.

Taylor briefly considered transferring to the University of Kansas. Luckily, he decided to stick it out. Although he was officially a starter again his junior year, at outside linebacker, Taylor couldn't seem to put together a whole game for the first five contests. On October 20, 1979, however, Taylor's football life suddenly burst into the forefront. The Tar Heels traveled to Raleigh, North Carolina, for a game against their archrivals at North Carolina State. As usual, it was a great game between the two foes and late in the fourth quarter, the Tar Heels held a 28-21 lead. State was marching downfield as the time ticked away. On second down, with the ball inside the Tar Heel 20, Taylor rushed toward the quarterback, who had dropped back to pass. With one ferocious hit, the ball was loose—a fumble—and UNC recovered. The home side argued that the play should have been called an incomplete forward pass. But the ref stood his ground and the Tar Heels raced upfield, scoring another touchdown for a 35-21 victory. Taylor's vicious hit was played over and over again on the sports reports on TV, both because of the hit itself and the controversy surrounding the referee's decision.

From that day on, Taylor was never short of confidence. Against Virginia late in the season, Taylor made nine tackles and assisted on two others to lead UNC to a 13-7 win. In addition, Taylor, who was named the league's Defensive Player of the Week, caused a fumble, intercepted a pass and made two tackles behind the line of scrimmage. A few weeks later, he followed up that effort with another one versus Michigan in

Coach Dick Crum got results out of Taylor. His Tar Heels put together a record of 11-1 in 1980.

the Gator Bowl. It was Taylor's fumble recovery late in the fourth quarter that helped forge the 17-15 victory in Jacksonville, Florida, before 70,407 fans. Earlier in the game, a Taylor sack stopped a key Michigan drive and put quarterback John Wangler on the sidelines with a broken leg.

UNC finished the 1979 campaign with a strong 8-3-1 record, including three wins in the final three games. Number 98 on the Tar Heels was Carolina's fourth-leading tackler with 80 solo hits and 15 assists. Eleven times he stopped opponents for losses, and he was tied for the team lead with five sacks. In addition, he caused seven fumbles. At the end of his junior year, Taylor hadn't made any all-star teams, but already pro scouts were pegging him as a can't-miss prospect.

Off the field, Taylor and his roommate and teammate Steve Streater used to challenge some of UNC's basketball players to pick-up games. Streater, who was all of 5' 8", and Taylor loved mixing it up with future superstars Michael Jordan and James Worthy. Taylor also met his future wife, Linda, in North Carolina.

When Taylor got to summer camp for his senior season, he had become a sleek 6' 3", 245-pounder. His teammates had a new nickname for their aggressive co-captain: Godzilla. With a defense that would be tops in the nation, the Tar Heels and Taylor got off to a rousing start, winning their first seven games. They beat Furman, Texas Tech, Maryland, Georgia Tech, Wake Forest, North Carolina State, and East Carolina with relative ease. With each week, Taylor's reputation got bigger and bigger. Against Texas Tech, Taylor's fumble recovery late in the game secured

a 9-3 verdict and against North Carolina State, there was one play where Taylor jumped over one blocker, then grabbed another and threw him into Wolfpack quarterback Tol Avery for a loss.

Bill Ard, who later played with Taylor on the New York Giants, remembers playing against Taylor while with Wake Forest. "I played against him for four years and with him for eight," says the former guard. "I'll never forget my senior year. That was a big game for us. We went in with a 3-1 record and North Carolina was 4-0. We ran a pro-style offense and we kept running pass plays. But Lawrence kept getting by the right guard who was supposed to pick him up and sacked our quarterback every other play it seemed. At halftime, our coach is yelling at the guy. 'Why can't you block that guy!' I said, 'Let me block him.' But I'm sure I couldn't have blocked him either. This was a guy who would become the greatest defensive player to play the game."

UNC's hopes for an undefeated season and a number one ranking were squashed in the eighth week of the season when a trip to Oklahoma resulted in a 41-7 pounding. But Sooner coach Barry Switzer voiced admiration for Taylor. "Taylor is a great, great player," he said. "Hugh Green is no better. Ross Browner is no better. He is the most active player we have ever seen." Sooner assistant coach Mervin Johnson added, "He looks like a rocket going to the ball."

Taylor played a key role in the following game, a 24-19 victory over Clemson, by sacking the Tiger quarterback deep in UNC territory with 30 seconds to go to seal the game. Three more wins followed, over Virginia, Duke, and Texas in the

Bluebonnet Bowl in Houston on December 31. In one incredible play in the bowl game that had pro scouts drooling, Taylor chased Herky Walls

60 yards to make a touchdown-saving tackle. By then, Taylor had a serious rep as someone who could— and would—make the big play.

UNC finished with a terrific 11-1 mark, matching the most wins in a season in school history. The Tar Heels won the ACC title for the first time since Taylor's freshman year. Taylor was a consensus All-American and the ACC Player of the Year. He, along with three other defenders—

Taylor helped lead the Tar Heels to a victory in the 1980 Bluebonnet Bowl. North Carolina beat the University of Texas by a score of 16-7.

Steve Streater, Darrell Nicolson, and Donnell Thompson—were named to the All-ACC first team. He had 55 solo tackles, six tackles behind the line of scrimmage, and 16 sacks for 127 yards in losses! He also forced three fumbles and recovered three others. A bona fide all-star, Taylor was picked to play in the East-West Shrine game (he played briefly before injuring his foot) and the Japan Bowl (he declined the invitation).

Even Crum, who had his share of run-ins with Taylor over the years, was amazed at his player's ability. "When you line up with Lawrence Taylor out there," he said, "you're lining up a man to play against boys."

4
NEW YORK, NEW YORK

Lawrence Taylor figured he was likely to go high in the National Football League draft. How high he didn't want to venture a guess. After all, there were some pretty good linebackers in the 1981 draft. Besides Taylor, it was expected that Hugh Green of Pittsburgh, the runner-up to George Rogers of South Carolina for the Heismann Trophy award, and All-America E. J. Junior of Alabama would go high. Ricky Jackson of Pittsburgh was highly touted, too. Of the bunch, Taylor probably had the least amount of national press in college.

When April 28, 1981—draft day—finally arrived, Taylor gathered with his friends in Chapel Hill to watch the proceedings on television. A few weeks earlier he had met with the head coach of New Orleans, Bum Phillips. Word had it that the Saints, who had the first pick, were torn between Rogers and Taylor.

Taylor made a quick impact on the Giants. Here he chases New York Jets quarterback Richard Todd.

The Saints took Rogers. Next up were the New York Giants, who were coming off a 4-12 campaign and a last place finish in the NFC East. Pundits had observed that the Giants had a fine defense and needed to fill offensive slots. Taylor headed for the kitchen for a beer.

When Taylor returned to the living room, he discovered he was a Giant. Ten minutes later Taylor got a phone call from coach Ray Perkins and that evening he was in the Meadowlands of New Jersey, meeting the staff and team officials. The following morning, Taylor was introduced to a throng of New York-area media.

"I'm happy to be going to New York because it's one of the greatest cities in the world," said Taylor. "There are so many people who can see you and appreciate you. I hope to bring the New York people a winner because that's something they deserve."

Taylor's euphoria during one of his first visits to New York would be shattered not long after. In rookie camp, he learned that his good friend Steve Streater, who was trying to make the Washington Redskins team, had been paralyzed in a car accident. Taylor, clearly upset, bolted from the camp for home where he went to see Streater. It was a rough time for the two friends, with Streater finally telling his buddy to get out and make things happen.

Meanwhile, back in New York, Taylor's arrival was met with some controversy. The Giants already had a solid linebacking crew that included Harry Carson in the middle and Brian Kelley and Brad Van Pelt outside. When Taylor signed a huge contract, immediately there were some rumblings.

"We felt like we already had a pretty good linebacking group," says Carson. "We didn't see the need to pick a linebacker that high in the draft. When Lawrence was drafted we knew he'd make big bucks. Yeah, our egos were bruised a little bit when we heard what he had signed for. But we also knew that it wasn't Lawrence. It was the system."

The Giants coaching staff recognized the quality of the linebackers they had. Instead of sitting or trading one of them, they revamped the whole defensive alignment. They removed a defensive lineman from their scheme, moved Kelley to the inside next to Carson, and put Taylor in Kelley's old spot on the outside, giving New York a 3-4 set-up.

"We were playing a 4-3 rather effectively," says Carson. "They couldn't take anybody's place so they compensated by going to a 3-4. As it turned out, they put LT in a position that maximized his skills and he became a super player. With his speed he was able to pressure the quarterback and also run people down from the backside."

It didn't take long for the veteran linebackers—and the rest of the team—to accept Taylor. Any lingering resentment was extinguished by the end of the first week of summer practice at Pace College.

"It didn't take long," Carson remembers. "The first practice you could tell he was going to be the man. He was third team the first day, second team the second and first team the next. It didn't take long to see that he was something special."

"Within three weeks of training camp he was blowing by everyone," adds Bill Ard, the Wake Forest guard who was drafted in 1981 as well.

"Nobody could touch him. You could tell he was a phenom."

In the team's first scrimmage, Taylor had four quarterback sacks and recovered a fumble. "I was doing what came naturally that afternoon,"

During rookie training camp, Taylor learned that his good friend Steve Streater, who was trying to make the Washington Redskins team, had been paralyzed in a car accident. Taylor bolted from camp and went to see Streater, who finally told his buddy to get back and make things happen.

Taylor reflected in his book. "I played with enthusiasm—like a lot of other new players." In the Giants' first preseason game, against the Chicago Bears at Soldier Field, he had 10 solo tackles, two sacks, and he recovered a loose ball in a game won by the Giants, 23-7.

By the start of the season, Taylor was entrenched as a member of the Giants' linebacking crew. In his first regular season game, Taylor served notice to a national TV audience that he was for real. In a game New York lost to the Eagles, 24-10, at Giants Stadium, Taylor decked Philadelphia quarterback Ron Jaworski on a blindside hit that had the sellout crowd stunned. The only problem was the refs deemed it a late hit, so the aggressive rookie earned his first professional roughing penalty on the same play.

Even though the Giants lost three of their first five games, people were beginning to forget the previous year's debacle and had high hopes for the season. And the defense, which had yielded 425 points in 1981, got tighter. The linebacking unit, with Taylor's presence, was even stronger than before.

"He made us a better group," said Carson. "He had an impact on us because people were focusing on him. That took the pressure off the rest of us and allowed us to play our positions with more freedom."

Everything began to click for the Giants in their sixth game, a win over the St. Louis Cardinals, and three weeks later they completed a three-game winning streak by beating the Atlanta Falcons, 27-24. It was a nasty day in Atlanta, with the weather cold and rainy and the field muddy. The Falcons took an early 17-7 lead but the Giants came back to tie the game in regulation. In the overtime, New York won it on a short Joe Danelo field goal. One of the highlights of the contest occurred late in the fourth quarter and it was Taylor who was in the middle of it. Carson remembers the play like it was yesterday. "Lawrence is rushing the quarterback and [blocking back] Lynn Cain caught Lawrence low and raised him up. So here's Lawrence doing a somersault in midair and you just hear the crowd going ooooohhhhh." On the next play, Taylor paid back Cain by smashing him as he tried to get outside with the ball. Cain left the field on a stretcher.

The Giants stumbled the next three weeks, losing three games, but over the last few weeks, the Giants shocked the football fraternity and found themselves in a position to make the playoffs as a wild-card team. On the last Sunday of the year the Giants did their part, defeating the Dallas Cowboys 13-10 in overtime on a snowy, windy day in Giants Stadium to end the campaign at 9-7. The next night, the New York Jets, who share Giants Stadium with the Giants, did their part for their neighbors, knocking off Green Bay. The Giants had made the playoffs for the first time in 18 years!

New York beat Philadelphia, the 1980 NFC champ, in the wild-card game. However, the book closed on their Cinderella season at the hands of San Francisco, 38-24, two days after the new year.

After the season, Taylor received several awards, including the league's Rookie of the Year. He was also a unanimous choice for the Pro Bowl. Taylor led the Giants in tackles with 133 and recorded a team-high 9½ sacks (which did not become an official NFL statistic until 1982). Most telling of Taylor's impact is the fact that the Giants gave up 168 fewer points than the year before.

In just one season Taylor had become somewhat of a legend. San Francisco realized that it needed something extra to block out Taylor and became the first team to use an interior lineman to block the linebacker in their playoff game. As Taylor says in his book, "I was never again allowed to play battering ram with tight ends and blocking backs." Indeed, in future years, other teams would follow suit, trying alternative blocking methods on Taylor.

"He changed the way people played defense—and offense," says Ard. "He changed teams' blocking schemes. Lawrence was too good a linebacker."

Around the league, there were only words of awe about Taylor. "I can't say enough about Taylor," offered Cardinals coach Jim Hanifan near the end of the regular season. "I don't think I've ever seen a kid who looks less like a rookie and more like an All-Pro. I don't mean to take anything away from their other linebackers. I always thought Harry Carson and Brad Van Pelt were among the best I've seen, but this kid, he's beyond description."

Taylor's teammates agreed. "Lawrence is probably the greatest athlete I've ever been associated with," said cornerback Terry Jackson. "He's probably the most dominant player out there."

"I've seen quarterbacks look at Lawrence and forget the snap count," added safety Beasley Reece. "You can tell when he's going to rush— it's like he's got a siren on his helmet."

Former Giants strength coach Jim Williams declared, "There may be some stronger linebackers, there may be some quicker. There may even be some more intelligent, but there are none who combine his strength, speed and smarts. No one knows how to stop the guy."

As for Taylor, he understated his initial season by giving the most of the credit to others. "I did pretty good for a rookie. But I feel anybody who works around guys like Van Pelt, Kelley, and Carson could look good—a 12th rounder would look good with these guys. They have been a tremendous help to me."

Yet even he had to admit that he was something special. "Anybody can tell when I'm coming, even in college they could," Taylor said. "But they still have to stop me. I like it when the offense has to worry about me. They have enough to worry about and thinking about me makes their job even more difficult. I'm pretty satisfied with my play so far but it could always be better."

Amazingly, he did get better. . . and better. . . and better.

The Giants' linebacking crew was feared around the league. Two nicknames given to (left to right) Lawrence Taylor, Harry Carson, Brad Van Pelt, and Brian Kelley were "The Crunch Bunch" and "the Board of De-wreckers."

5
SUPERHUMAN AND ALL TOO HUMAN

Lawrence Taylor may have caught some teams by surprise his rookie year, but by the first game of his sophomore season, Taylor had no such luck. "In my rookie year I was able to take people by surprise," Taylor said in an interview for *Sport Magazine*. "By my second season they were all over me. All of a sudden all the focus was on me. The press was all over me, opposing players all trying to take my head off. I decided to low key-it, maybe try and sneak up on 'em. Didn't work."

He had all the confidence on the field but still had a lot to learn. He admitted that he didn't know one city from the next. He brought mud cleats for a game in Seattle because teammates Brad Van Pelt and Brian Kelley told him it rains a lot there. Taylor's jaw dropped when they arrived at Seattle's domed stadium.

Taylor, along with Leonard Marshall, celebrates yet another powerful hit, this one leveling Philadelphia Eagles quarterback Ron Jaworski.

In the 1982 preseason, Taylor injured a foot, which slowed him down considerably. An impending players' strike slowed everyone down on the squad. The Giants lost to the Atlanta Falcons, 16-14, to open the season. Eight days later, on a Monday night, the Giants went down again, 27-19 to the Green Bay Packers. There were a number of bad omens that night in Giants Stadium, starting with the lights going out twice during the game and the fans taking their frustration out on both teams because of the strike, which by then, was expected to go into effect following the game.

And sure enough, the next morning the NFL season was halted. What was expected to be a short break turned longer and longer, lasting eight weeks in all. Taylor, like everybody else, went home, spending time with Linda, now his wife, and their son, T. J. It didn't take long for Taylor to tire of the routine because, after all, it was the fall and the fall meant football. So he was greatly relieved when the season finally resumed.

Of course, the 70,000 fans who jammed Giants Stadium for the first game back might have thought differently as New York fell to 0-3 in losing to the Washington Redskins. Worse, afterwards, Taylor was told he wouldn't start later in the week against Detroit by defensive coach Bill Parcells, who felt the foot injury was still flaring up and slowing him down. Naturally, Taylor had his own opinion, which was that he was perfectly fine and should start.

In Detroit for a Thanksgiving Day match-up, Taylor did not start but he was back in full time by the end of the second quarter. In the third quarter, the Taylor everyone remembered from a year before emerged again. He sacked quarterback Gary Danielson to stop one scoring threat and then in the fourth quarter made a highlight-film-type play with the Lions on the verge of scoring and breaking a 6-6 tie.

"They were running this play with Danielson trying to throw to the fullback [Horace King]," remembers Giant guard Bill Ard. "But LT made the interception and ran 97 yards for a touchdown." It was the kind of play, adds Ard, that ordinary players don't ever make.

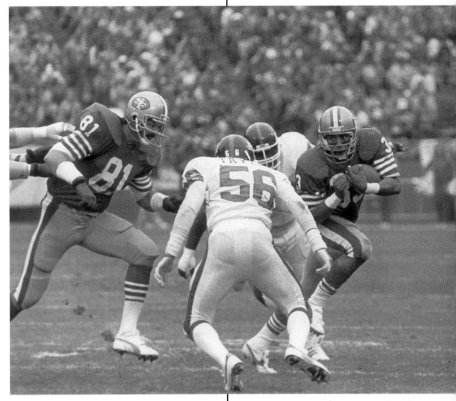

San Francisco running back Roger Craig jukes around Lawrence Taylor as the 49ers ended the Giants playoff hopes in 1984.

"I ran and ran and ran," Taylor wrote in his book. "I was worried about getting hauled down from behind. Each time I turned I got a quick look at someone running stride for stride with me. At the Detroit 20, I realized it was my own shadow." Taylor finished his 97-yard jaunt by hook sliding into the end zone.

Although the Giants won their next two games, they were out of the playoff race soon after. They finished a disappointing 4-5 in the strike-shortened season. Taylor, however, was again named to the Pro Bowl and as the Defensive Player of

In one of football's most notorious moments, Taylor sacks Washington quarterback Joe Theisman. Theisman broke his leg and he never was the same afterward.

the Year, leading the Giants in sacks with 7 ½.

The biggest news of the season, it turned out, was the resignation of head coach Ray Perkins near the end of the campaign. Parcells was immediately named to replace Perkins.

"Bill was as different from Perk as night from day," Taylor commented in his book. In an interview for an article, he described Parcells as "more easygoing, more accessible to the players—a players' coach. Ray was more like a sergeant in the army."

The bumbling Giants took another step back the first year under Parcells, tumbling to 3-12-1 and finishing at the bottom of the NFC East. The team had problems all season long, mainly on offense. The Giants tried three quarterbacks, but Scott Brunner was erratic, Phil Simms broke a thumb, and Jeff Rutledge was both erratic and suffered an injury. The good news, if there was some, was that the defense was the third best in the NFL. And there was no doubt why the Giants defense was ranked so high.

By this time, Taylor was being compared with the best pass rushers of all time and was singled out as the best ever at getting to the quarterback. "There were times when I didn't know if I was supposed to be on the strong side or the weak side, so I said, 'I don't cover very well, but I rush pretty good, so I'm going to rush regardless,' " Taylor philosophized. "So I started rushing a lot and the coaches would get into the film the next day and say, 'You messed up again. You were supposed to drop, but good play, because you sacked him anyway.'"

And Taylor loved to sack the quarterback. "A sack is when you run up behind somebody who's not watching, he doesn't see you, and you really put your helmet into him. The ball goes fluttering everywhere and the coach comes out and asks the quarterback, 'Are you all right?' That's a sack."

His teammates continued to be in awe of him, too. "He was able to elevate his game as time went on," says Harry Carson. "During one on one drills we would sit on our helmets and just watch him. As he got older we got a kick watching him go up against a rookie lineman. You could see the fear in their eyes. It was like taking candy from a baby for Lawrence."

It seemed easy, maybe, but by this time Taylor was not only a dangerous defender because of his great speed, but because he was also taking a thinking man's approach to the game. As more and more teams set up blocking schemes to stop him, he came up with alternative moves to counteract them. More often than not, he was the winner of that week's particular battle. But it was not without some frustrating moments.

"I'd look at movies [of the other team] all week and then on Sunday they'd come up with something new," Taylor said. "It seems as if I was always chasing, chasing, chasing. I wish they'd just run my way once in a while so I could have some fun."

Taylor nearly didn't play the 1983 season. Looking for an extension on his contract, Taylor had sat out most of the preseason before he finally decided to rejoin the team after Giants management agreed to talk about the contract at the end of the season. Management's hand was forced late in the season, though, when representatives of Donald Trump, who owned the New Jersey Generals of the upstart United States Football League, contacted Taylor about jumping ship when his Giants contract was up. Eventually, Taylor was so impressed with Trump and his offer that he signed a deal. Naturally, the Giants were taken aback. In the weeks ahead, they not only paid off Trump to kill the contract, but they gave Taylor more money—and the extension on his contract.

During the off-season, the face of the Giants began to change. Brad Van Pelt and Brian Kelley were traded away as part of a general housecleaning effort. The Giants suddenly became a serious contender and a perennial playoff team. In 1984, they won three of their first four games and survived a two-game losing streak at the end of the season to take a wild-card spot in the playoffs. They nipped the Los Angeles Rams, 16-13, but San Francisco ended New York's playoff run for the second time in four years with a 21-10 verdict in chilly Candlestick Park.

In 1985, the Giants, sparked by a four-game winning streak midway through the campaign, again gained a wild-card spot when they went 10-6. The defense played masterfully and gained revenge on the 49ers in a 17-3 win at Giants

Stadium. A week later, however, the Giants were no match for the eventual Super Bowl winners, the Chicago Bears, losing 21-0 on a bone-chilling afternoon at Soldier Field.

In the eyes of many people, Taylor's 1985 season was overshadowed by one frozen moment in time. On November 18, the Giants were in RFK Stadium for a Monday night game against the Redskins. The second quarter had barely begun when Washington tried to pull off a trick play. Quarterback Joe Theisman took the snap from center and handed off to running back John Riggins. Riggins took a step forward and then tossed the ball back to Theisman. The 36-year old All-Pro quarterback skipped away from an onrushing Harry Carson but was caught by Taylor. The 240-pound Giants linebacker fell on Theisman as teammate Gary Reasons came in from the other side. Theisman crashed to the

Mark Bavaro looks as if he's going to catch the ball, but he deflected it and it ended up in the hands of Phil McConkey (right) for a touchdown. The Giants beat the Denver Broncos, 39-20, in the 1987 Super Bowl.

ground, his right leg twisted sideways beneath him, resulting in an ugly compound multiple fracture. Everyone on the field, including Taylor, knew the seriousness of the injury. Players from both teams immediately called for medical attention. "I had always heard stories about being able to hear a bone break across the field," Taylor wrote. "I could actually hear Joe's bone breaking. Then I saw his leg, what had happened, saw him rolling and rolling around in agony."

For Taylor, it was the eighth career sack of Theisman— and the last. Theisman made a brief comeback the following year, but was never the same. Soon he entered the broadcast booth, talking about football, not playing it.

In Taylor's mind, the 1985 season was troubling in another way. He had been using drugs on and off since 1982, but in the past couple of years his dependency had gotten worse. The superhuman football player had been reduced to simply human. By the end of the 1985 season, he was hooked on cocaine. He secretly went into a drug rehabilitation center and was admitted to different programs as he sought to clean himself up.

In the second quarter of the Super Bowl, George Martin (right) sacked quarterback John Elway in the end zone for a safety. Lawrence Taylor, Erik Howard, and Leonard Marshall were also there to celebrate and make sure Elway knew he was down.

He eventually came up with his own rehabilitation plan, one that had him playing a lot of golf and keeping busy with other activities. The secret got out, though, when sportscaster Howard Cosell revealed that Taylor had a drug problem and was in rehab. Taylor managed to keep away from the press for the rest of the off-season before the inevitable came at training camp. Parcells kept the press at bay, though, when he threatened to close the locker room for the season if they didn't stop bothering Taylor.

Throughout the 1986 season, Taylor seemed to take out his troubles on opposing teams. Following a season-opening loss to the Dallas Cowboys, the Giants, spurred by Taylor, reeled off five wins in a row. They lost to Seattle the next week. That would be the team's last loss of the year. The next week, the Giants beat Washington, 27-20, the first of 12 straight victories. The win over the Redskins put the Giants into a tie for first place and clearly was the key to the rest of the season. On the same late October Monday evening that the New York Mets beat the Boston Red Sox, 8-5, to win the seventh and deciding game of the World Series, Taylor was the main man for the Giants, coming up with five tackles and three sacks. In between plays, the 75,973 fans at Giants Stadium alternately cheered, "Let's Go Mets!" and "Defense, Defense," in reference to the Giants. For Taylor, it was the first of two great regular season games against Washington and in particular, against Redskin quarterback Jay Schroeder, who had the Giants all-star in his face every minute he was on the field. In the two games, Taylor accumulated 18 tackles and six sacks as the Giants posted a pair of important wins. Yet, his 23-tackle, seven-sack performance (including four in one game) in a pair of victories over Philadelphia may have been even more impressive.

The 1986 team was composed of many great players, not just Taylor. Phil Simms had a terrific year at quarterback, and Joe Morris broke team records for running backs. Hard-nosed but quiet Mark Bavaro rewrote the description of tight ends and the defense was buoyed by Carson and the 1984 first round draft choice, linebacker Carl Banks, as well as noseguard Jim Burt and defensive tackle Leonard Marshall.

In the first round of the playoffs, the Giants overwhelmed San Francisco, 49-3, in a game that featured a 34-yard interception return for a touchdown by Taylor and a hit by Burt that left quarterback Joe Montana unconscious. In the NFC championship game a week later, the Giants decked Washington for the third time, this time winning 17-0 and gaining a berth in the Super Bowl for the first time in the team's long history. Meanwhile, the Denver Broncos won the AFC title, setting up a Super Bowl showdown at the Rose Bowl in Pasadena, California, on January 25, 1987.

There's nothing like being a part of the Super Bowl and Taylor felt the excitement like everyone else. The Giants stayed in a hotel in Costa Mesa and no matter what time of day it was, the place was mobbed with tourists and media people. When he wasn't at practice at the Rams' Anaheim complex, Taylor mostly stayed in his room to avoid the crush, laying low and watching a lot of television. Even for a guy who liked to party, this was too much for him.

What the Giants needed to do in order to beat the Broncos was no secret. They had to stop their scrambling, strong-armed quarterback, John

Elway. "The biggest thing we have to do," said Taylor, "is to take care of John Elway. We have a lot of respect for him."

On a sunny and warm day in front of 101,063 spectators at the Rose Bowl and millions more on TV, Phil Simms, not John Elway, did the most impressive improvising, completing 22 of 25 passes for 268 yards and three touchdowns as New York broke open a close game in the second half for a convincing 39-20 victory. Trailing 10-9 at the half, New York scored 24 unanswered points in the third period behind Simms, who was named the game's MVP, to take a commanding lead. Carl Banks was the defensive star for the Giants, racking up 10 solo tackles. For Taylor, it wasn't close to his best game. Yet it didn't matter to him. The important thing was the win—a Super Bowl win. So when the Giants celebrated by hoisting the Super Bowl trophy high in the air in their locker room afterwards, there was an elated Lawrence Taylor hoisting it too.

It wasn't the only award Taylor hoisted at the end of the season, a season that had Taylor setting an all-time Giants record for sacks with 20½ and recording 105 total tackles and three forced fumbles. He was the unanimous selection choice as the NFL's Most Valuable Player, the first time a defensive player had won that award since Alan Page of the Minnesota Vikings had done the trick ten years earlier. In addition, he was a unanimous All-NFL choice and a unanimous Pro Bowl selection and starter for the sixth consecutive year. He won the Maxwell Trophy, was the Kansas City 101 winner, and received the Seagrams Award. In a career that included so many great years, 1986 may have been the greatest of them all.

6

ONE OF
THE GREATS

For Lawrence Taylor and his Giants teammates, the euphoria of the 1986 season had barely worn off when talk of another strike began to
surface. As it turned out, the strike would be
the first of many trying experiences for Taylor
over the next few years. Late in the 1987 season
he missed his first game because of an injury—
ever. He played hurt with a hamstring injury for
a couple of weeks and finally gave in to the pain
by taking a week off. Over the next few years,
injuries would hamper him—although not nec-
essarily stop him—at one time or another. And
in 1988, Taylor was suspended for four games
at the start of the year when he tested positive
for substance abuse. Trying times for Taylor,
indeed.

The 1987 season was basically a wash for the
Giants. After winning the Super Bowl, they lost

*In 1992, Taylor held a press conference to announce
that he had formed a sports drink company and was
about to introduce "LT's Metro Pro." Taylor's six-
year-old daughter, Paula, stayed close to his side.*

the first five games of the year (including two strike games played with replacement players) and finished a disappointing 6-9. In 1988, things got better as the Giants went 10-6, good for second place in the NFC East, but not good enough to make the playoffs. In one memorable game in November, Taylor played perhaps his most courageous game.

New York was in New Orleans for a contest against the Saints. The Giants were beat up. Phil Simms was out with a sprained shoulder, Carl Banks was out with a sprained knee, and Taylor was slowed by a torn shoulder muscle. With the playoffs still within reach, however, Taylor was not about to sit this one out. Despite playing in extreme pain, literally picking himself up off the artificial turf time and time again, Taylor recorded three sacks, two forced fumbles and seven tackles to lead the Giants to a 13-12 win. Taylor, showing his incredible ability to withstand pain, played with an injury that would have sidelined the average player, taking a break only to give the shoulder a moment's rest. "It kept tearing every play, a little more each time," Taylor grimaced afterwards.

Defensive coordinator Bill Belichick commented, "Lawrence was playing in a lot of pain. It was excruciating. You could see it on the bench. It was a courageous effort." Added offensive lineman Karl Nelson, "It's like you scrape Lawrence off the field, give him one play to rest on the sidelines, then send him back in there."

In 1989, Taylor assumed the role of co-captain of the Giants, replacing the retired Harry Carson. With the help of his leadership, New York posted a 12-4 record and vaulted to a first place finish in the division. But the Giants stum-

bled in the first round of the playoffs, losing to the Los Angeles Rams 19-13 in overtime at Giants Stadium. On the game's final play, Ram wide receiver Flipper Anderson caught a pass, raced into the end zone for the winning touchdown, and continued running through the tunnel straight to the locker room, stunning the crowd of 76,325 into a dead silence.

In 1990, Taylor missed almost all of the preseason as he and his agent were bogged down in contract talks with Giants management. Five days before the opener, Taylor inked a new deal. Three practices later, he told the astonished

Taylor was slowed by several injuries in the late years of his career, but he could still be a major force when necessary. Here he takes down Washington Redskin running back Earnest Byner, with a little help from Pepper Johnson.

press—and an even more astonished Coach Parcells, that he was ready to go. While he did not play the whole first game against the Philadelphia Eagles, he played enough to drive Randall Cunningham crazy. Taylor constantly pressured the multitalented Eagle quarterback, sacking him three times. He also racked up seven tackles and forced the Eagles to change their offensive game plan. "I keep hearing how old I am," Taylor had said a couple of weeks earlier, in reference to general manager George Young's reluctance to pay big dollars for someone he perceived as being too old. "I don't need a cane or anything."

The Giants continued to roll over the next two months or so, winning their first 10 games of the year—in most cases, in a breeze. They rebounded from a two-game losing streak by winning three of their last four games. For the second year in a row, the Giants finished first in the division, one-upping themselves with a 13-3 record.

There were to be no playoff disappointments this year. New York whipped Chicago 31-3 in the NFC semi-final round and came from behind to nip San Francisco in an exciting conference championship game, 15-13. Taylor's recovery of a Roger Craig fumble late in the game nailed down the win and a date with the Buffalo Bills for Super Bowl XXV in Tampa Stadium in Florida. The fumble recovery was a big moment for Taylor, whose statistics weren't among his best during the regular season. While he had a team-high 10½ sacks, he had one stretch where he had just two in over 10 weeks. And there were a couple of games in which Taylor couldn't seem to deliver as he once had, rather turning it on, it seemed, in spurts.

Taylor would have liked to have had bigger numbers heading into the Super Bowl, but he wasn't worked up about it. The important thing was that he was back for the biggest game in America.

The usual fervor was encountered by game time, even with the United States military taking front page headlines with their involvement in a war in the Middle East against Iraq. At kickoff, at least for a few hours, Americans would try and forget what was going on in the Gulf War, instead looking forward to a great time for what many expected to be a great game between a team, the Giants, with an outstanding defense, against another team, the Bills, who were known for a fast-paced offense led by quarterback Jim Kelly. Oddsmakers favored the Bills, who had steamrollered their opposition in the AFC. After all, Phil Simms was unavailable to play due to an injury, and the Giants' lead runner was the aged veteran Ottis Anderson. Meanwhile, the Bills had the dynamic Thurman Thomas to run the ball for them, along with All-Pro receiver Andre Reed.

For one of the few times in the history of the game, the advanced billing lived up to its hype. The game was a thriller.

Bill Parcell's master plan called for the Giants to keep the ball in their offense's hands as long as possible. Without the ball, the Bills offensive threat was of limited use. The Giants' defense, which went into several once-in-a-lifetime formations in order to stop the Bills' heralded no-huddle offense, played well. But it was the offense that really excelled. The Giants, behind MVP Ottis Anderson's 102 rushing yards and quarterback Jeff Hostetler's 20-32 for 222 yard performance, set an all-time Super Bowl record with 40:33 possession time.

The Bills jumped to a 12-3 lead, but the gutsy Giants bounced back to make the score 17-12 in their favor. With time running down, Buffalo scored a touchdown on one of their patented quick strikes, but the Giants ground out a long drive and Matt Bahr capped it with a field goal to give the Giants a late 20-19 lead.

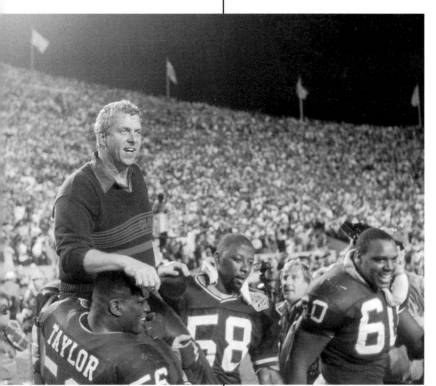

In one of the grittiest of Super Bowls, the Giants eked out a win over the Buffalo Bills, 20-19, in 1991. Taylor and Carl Banks lift up Coach Bill Parcells after Scott Norwood's last-second field goal attempt drifted wide.

With only seconds left on the clock and 73,813 delirious fans screaming, Kelly rushed the offense downfield and turned the ball over to their kicker, Scott Norwood. Norwood's 47-yard field goal attempt just missed as the clock expired.

Following the Super Bowl victory, big changes invaded the Giants' world. Bill Parcells resigned and was replaced by assistant coach Ray Handley. Under Handley, the next two years were disastrous for the Giants, who were a lackluster 8-8 and 6-10. Taylor considered retirement—for personal reasons—prior to the 1992 season and hinted that it would be his last year. "There was a time when I was playing football that every minute of every day, all I thought about was football—making this tackle and making that tackle. Every now and then, I'd think about a golf shot. But now it's starting to turn the other way, and I think about golf a lot," he said.

Taylor, feeling more secure with himself at that point in time, added, "I've got my life on the right track. I was straying away for awhile, but I've worked hard in the last couple of years to change my image somewhat in certain areas, and to put myself in a more positive light." And a few weeks into the season, Taylor acknowledged that it would be his last season. And he would have retired, had he not suffered an Achilles tendon injury and missed the last six weeks of the season. "Nobody wants to go out with an injury," he said. "Nobody wants to leave the game on somebody's else's terms."

And so Taylor came back for one more year—and another coach. Former Denver Bronco coach Dan Reeves was hired to replace Handley. The Giants responded to the change by taking second place in the division with an 11-5 mark. New York stopped the Minnesota Vikings, 17-10, in the wild-card game, before getting bombed by the San Francisco 49ers, 44-3. Afterwards, in the visiting locker room at Candlestick Park, Taylor made it official. He was retiring. His illustrious career was over. He told a throng of reporters that he was retiring "because I've done everything I can do. I've been to Super Bowls, I've been to the playoffs, I've been able to do things in this game that haven't been done before. I've earned the respect of players and people in general around the country. So that's all you want to do when you pick a career, and that's what I've done."

Taylor, sweat still dripping onto his white jersey with the number 56 on it, eyed the members

Since retiring, and while waiting to become eligible for the Pro Football Hall of Fame, Taylor spends a lot of his time playing golf.

of the press through dark sunglasses. "I'm going to miss just being around the guys because I've been playing organized sports with the New York Giants for 13 years," continued the 34-year old legend, now fingering the "LT" earring hanging from his left ear. "It's just like a family to me. I'm closer to my teammates than I am with other people in the real world. I'm think I'm as good as 90 percent of the linebackers in the game, but that's not what I'm looking at. I've put in my time. I'm glad it's over. Hey, I deserve a rest."

Taylor's last act on the playing field came moments after the game had ended. He ran out to ask Referee Bernie Kukar for his yellow flag. "I wanted his flag," Taylor explained with a smile, because "he's thrown it against me enough."

Opponents only wish that Taylor had smiled a bit more often at them. But he didn't, except perhaps after coming up with the big play—a sack, a fumble recovery or the game-saving tackle. But then, it was more like a sneer. In 13 years, he did a lot of sneering, recording 132.5 sacks (actually, it was 142 if you include 9.5 in his rookie year when the stat was not official), second behind all-time leader Reggie White. A perennial Pro Bowler, Taylor was the Defensive Player of the Week nine times, the Defensive Player of the Month twice, and in 1989, was a unanimous choice to the NFL's All-1980s team.

Around the league, there were only words of praise for Taylor upon his retirement. Ron

Jaworski of the Eagles, who was sacked 12.5 times by Taylor (tying Randall Cunningham as the linebacker's main victims), noted, "He was simply the most dynamic player I ever faced." Neil Lomax, the former St. Louis Cardinals quarterback who was sacked 12 times, said "We'd run at him, we'd throw at him, we'd have three guys on him. It didn't seem to matter."

San Francisco lineman Steve Wallace indicated that "it was a nightmare when you played a guy like that in an open field." Jerry Sisemore, who played tackle for the Eagles from 1973-1984 added, "There were many sleepless nights because you played New York twice a year. Toward the middle of the week something would come over you and you'd just start sweating. My last year in the league, opening day, he immediately got past me. I just sort of rolled and he tripped. He just looked at me and laughed. Right there I thought I had to get out of this game."

Perhaps it was Joe Theisman who had the most revealing compliment for Taylor. "You just couldn't go through the motions. He was the ultimate pass-rushing machine. When I dropped back, the first thing I did was to glance over my left shoulder to see if he was coming. If he was dropping back in coverage, a sense of calm came over me. If he was coming, I had a sense of urgency."

Closer to home, Bill Parcells said "when people talk about who was the best outside linebacker, they're not going to put him in a group with seven or eight others. The bus station is full of guys who were going to be the next Lawrence Taylor."

There seems to be only one more logical step for Taylor, now the father of three (Paula, Tanisha, and T.J.): The Football Hall of Fame in Canton, Ohio. A former Giant and Hall of Famer, linebacker Sam Huff, said midway through Taylor's career, "[He] is the most dominating player in the game and right up there with the best of all time. If you were designing an offense, Jim Brown would be the runner. If you were designing a defense, LT would be the prototype linebacker."

Longtime teammate Harry Carson sums up Taylor's chances for making the Hall of Fame this way: "He's the best. No question. I don't think anyone would argue that. He is simply head and shoulders above everybody else."

Not bad for a kid who didn't know what the game of football was about until it was almost too late.

STATISTICS

LAWRENCE TAYLOR

New York Giants

Year	ST	AT	TOTAL	SACKS	FF	FR	INT	TD
1981	94	39	133	9.5	2	1	1	0
1982	32	23	55	7.5	2	1	1	1
1983	88	37	125	9.0	0	2	2	0
1984	88	26	114	11.5	4	0	1	0
1985	83	21	104	13.0	4	2	0	0
1986	79	26	105	20.5	2	0	0	0
1987	53	9	62	12.0	2	0	3	0
1988	65	8	73	15.5	3	1	0	0
1989	65	18	83	15.0	4	0	0	0
1990	64	20	84	10.5	3	1	1	1
1991	52	15	67	7.0	2	2	0	0
1992	36	11	47	5.0	2	1	0	0
1993	29	7	36	6.0	3	1	0	0
Totals	828	260	1088	142.0	33	12	9	2

Postseason

Year	ST	AT	TOTAL	SACKS	FF	FR	INT	TD
1981	6	6	12	2.0	0	0	0	0
1984	11	1	12	3.0	1	0	0	0
1985	15	4	19	1.0	0	0	0	0
1986	6	6	12	0.0	0	0	1	1
1989	5	2	7	2.0	1	0	0	0
1990	5	2	7	0.5	0	1	0	0
1993	2	3	5	0.0	0	0	0	0
totals	50	24	74	8.5	2	1	1	1

ST   solo tackles
AT   assisted tackles
FF   fumbles forced
FR   fumbles recovered
INT   interceptions
TD   touchdowns

LAWRENCE TAYLOR
A CHRONOLOGY

1959 Lawrence Taylor born in Williamsburg, Virginia, on February 4

1977 Announces his intention to attend the University of North Carolina

1980 Named the Atlantic Coast Conference Player of the Year

1981 Drafted by the New York Giants in the first round of the NFL draft, the second player overall picked

1986 Named the NFL's Most Valuable Player; leads league in sacks with 20.5

1987 Helps lead the Giants to their first-ever Super Bowl win, a 39-20 victory over the Denver Broncos

1991 Helps lead the Giants to their second Super Bowl win, 20-19 over the Buffalo Bills

1993 Announces his retirement

SUGGESTIONS FOR FURTHER READING

Burt, Jim, with Hank Gola, *Hard Nose*. San Diego, Harcourt, Brace, Jovanovich, 1987.

Garber, Angus, G., III, *Football Legends*. New York, Gallery Books, 1988.

Izenberg, Jerry, *No Medals for Trying: A Week in the Life of a Pro Football Team*. New York, Macmillan, 1990.

Nelson, Karl, with Barry Stanton, *Life on the Line*. New York, WRS Publishing, 1993.

Simms, Phil, and McConkey, Phil, with Dick Schaap. *Simms to McConkey*. Crown Publishing, 1987.

Stanton, Barry, "Sport Interview." Sport Magazine, November, 1985.

Taylor, Lawrence, *Living on the Edge*. New York, Times Books, 1987.

ABOUT THE AUTHOR

Dan Hirshberg is the Executive Editor for North Jersey Newspapers, Hackettstown, N.J., and is the author of *Phil Rizzuto: A Yankee Tradition*, as well as books on Emmitt Smith and John Elway for Chelsea House. He lives in Hackettstown with his wife, Susan, and two children, Nathan and Melanie.

INDEX

Anderson, Flipper, 53
Anderson, Ottis, 12, 55
Ard, Bill, 28, 33, 36, 41
Avery, Tol, 28
Bahr, Matt, 12, 56
Banks, Carl, 48, 49, 52, 56
Bavaro, Mark, 45, 48
Belichick, Bill, 52
Browner, Ross, 29
Brunner, Scott, 42
Bucci, Mike, 19–21
Burt, Jim, 48
Byner, Earnest, 53
Cain, Lynn, 35
Carson, Harry, 32, 33, 34, 36, 37, 43, 45, 48, 52, 60
Cosell, Howard, 47
Craig, Roger, 41, 54
Crum, Dick, 25, 29
Cunningham, Randall, 53, 59
Danelo, Joe, 35
Danielson, Gary, 40
Dooley, Bill, 23, 24, 25
Elway, John, 46, 49
Fox, Mike, 12
Gannon, Rich, 11, 12
Gray, Mel, 21
Handley, Ray, 56, 57
Hanifan, Jim, 36
Hardison, Dee, 24, 25
Hostetler, Jeff, 55
Howard, Erik, 46
Huff, Sam, 60
Jackson, Greg, 12
Jackson, Ricky, 31
Jackson, Terry, 37
Jaworski, Ron, 34, 38, 59

Johnson, Billy, 24
Johnson, Marvin, 29
Johnson, Pepper, 53
Jones, Melvin, 18, 20, 21
Jordan, Michael, 27
Junior, E. J., 31
Kelley, Brian, 32, 33, 37, 39, 44
Kelly, Jim, 55, 56
King, Horace, 41
Kukar, Bernie, 58
Lomax, Neil, 59
Mansfield, Mike, 21
Marshall, Leonard, 39, 46, 48
Martin, George, 46
McConkey, Phil, 45
McConnel, Tony, 19
McDaniels, T. K., 24
Montana, Joe, 48
Morris, Joe, 48
Nelson, Karl, 52
Nicholson, Darrell, 25, 29
Norwood, Scott, 56
Parcells, Bill, 13, 40, 42, 47, 53, 55, 56, 59
Perkins, Ray, 32, 41
Phillips, Bum, 31
Reasons, Gary, 12
Reece, Beasley, 37
Reeves, Dan, 57
Riggins, John, 45
Rogers, George, 31
Rutledge, Jeff, 42
Schroeder, Jay, 47
Sheets, Kenny, 24
Simms, Phil, 42, 48, 49, 52, 55

Springs, Ron, 20, 21
Streater, Steve, 27, 29, 32, 34
Switzer, Barry, 29
Taylor, Buddy, 15–16
Taylor, Clarence, 16
Taylor, Kim, 16
Taylor, Lawrence
  as a baseball player, 15, 17
  as a basketball player, 23
  honors received, 26, 29, 36, 41, 49, 52, 58
  injuries of, 25, 39, 51, 52, 57
  nicknames of, 25, 27, 37
Taylor, Linda, 40
Taylor, Paula, 51, 59
Taylor, T. J., 40, 60
Taylor, Tanisha, 59
Theisman, Joe, 42, 45–46, 59
Thomas, Betsy, 18
Thomas, Thurman, 55
Thompson, Donnell, 28
Todd, Richard, 31
Trump, Donald, 44
Van Pelt, Brad, 32, 36, 37, 39, 44
Walker, Herschel, 10
Walls, Herky, 29
Wallace, Steve, 59
Wangler, John 27
White, Reggie, 58
Williams, Jim 37
Worthy, James, 27
Young, George, 54